Listen to Your Fish

Terrific Tips for Pet Care

By Sarah Albee
Illustrated by Tom Brannon

Published by Creative Edge, 2010, an imprint of Dalmatian _____ _____67. No part of this book may be reproduced or copied in any form without writte_____ _____ 1-800-815-8696

Printed _____

CE12919/0410/ZHE

D1377183

Pet Rule #1: Do give your pet fresh food and clean water every day.

Pet Rule #2: Do make sure your pet gets regular checkups at the veterinarian.

Pet Rule #3: Do be sure your pet gets exercise every day.

Pet Rule #4: Do help your pet stay clean and well-groomed.

Pet Rule #6: Do not go near strange dogs . . . or crocodiles.

Pet Rule #7: Do keep your pet on a leash in public places.

CATNIP